What Time Is It?

By Susan Ring

CELEBRATION PRESS
Pearson Learning Group

The following people from **Pearson Learning Group**
have contributed to the development of this product:

Joan Mazzeo **Design** | **Editorial** Leslie Feierstone Barna, Teri Crawford Jones
Christine Fleming **Marketing** | **Publishing Operations** Jennifer Van Der Heide
Production Laura Benford-Sullivan
Content Area Consultants Dr. Amy Rabb-Liu and Dr. Charles Liu

The following people from **DK** have
contributed to the development of this product:

Art Director Rachael Foster
Martin Wilson **Managing Art Editor** | **Managing Editor** Marie Greenwood
Jo Dixon **Design** | **Editorial** Jennie Morris
Helen McFarland **Picture Research** | **Production** Gordana Simakovic
Richard Czapnik, Andy Smith **Cover Design** | **DTP** David McDonald
Consultant Keith Lye

Dorling Kindersley would like to thank: Marian Broderick for additional research; Shirley Cachia and Rose Horridge in the DK Picture Library; Andy Crawford for new photography; Jo Dixon for original artwork; Ed Merritt in DK Cartography; Johnny Pau for additional cover design work; Philip Wilkinson for additional consultancy; and model Naadirah Qazi.

Picture Credits: Corbis: 22br, 28bcr; Paul Almasy 20cr, 28bl; Bettmann 25br; Jonathan Blair 29t; Sheldan Collins 20b; Archivio Iconographico, S.A. 19t; David Higgs 13tr; Bob Krist 11; Araldo de Luca 18; Roger Ressmeyer 1. DK Images: Anglo Australian Observatory 7; National Maritime Museum 23bc, 28br; Science Museum 22bc. Getty Images: Robin Smith 13tl. NASA: 8c, 10l, 12bc. National Maritime Museum, London: 15br. Nature Picture Library: Heikki Willamo/Naturbild 27cr. Photolibrary.com: IFA - Bilderteam GMBH 4–5. Seapics.com: Mark V. Erdmann 26br. Topfoto: Science Museum/HIP 21tr. Cover: Corbis: front tr; Paul Almasy front b.

All other images: DK Dorling Kindersley © 2005. For further information see www.dkimages.com

ISBN: 0-7652-5233-3

Color reproduction by Colourscan, Singapore
Printed in the United States of America
2 3 4 5 6 7 8 9 10   08 07 06 05 04

1-800-321-3106
www.pearsonlearning.com

Contents

Keeping Track of Time

What time is it? Most people ask that question many times a day. People don't want to be late for class or early for a visit. They don't want to wake up too early or go to bed too late. Favorite television shows or celebrations usually happen at a certain time or on certain days. Clocks and calendars help people keep track of what time and day it is.

Ancient peoples looked to the seasons to measure the passage of time. They also determined time by the rising and setting of the Sun. People knew that when the Sun came up in the morning, it was time for a new day.

The rising of the Sun still signals the start of a new day for most people, although midnight is the official start.

A watch or a clock shows us how much time has passed. Nature also displays the results of time passing. People grow older. Little cubs grow into huge bears, and tiny seeds grow into tall trees.

From the use of sundials to the most complicated electric and **atomic clocks**, humans have attempted to keep track of time for centuries. This book explains how people have calculated time over the ages. It also explains how time as we measure it relates to the universe and our solar system. A section at the end of the book answers some common questions about time and provides a timeline that summarizes the history of telling time.

Time and Space

When Time Began

Many scientists think that our universe began between 10 and 15 billion years ago with an enormous explosion in space called the **Big Bang**. Our universe is believed to have come into existence at the moment the Big Bang occurred. Space began to expand, and time started to pass.

Billions of years after the Big Bang, our solar system formed. The solar system consists of the Sun, the planets, moons, and other objects such as comets and asteroids. It is part of an even bigger system, a galaxy called the Milky Way. About every 200 million years, the solar system revolves around the center of the galaxy.

This photo shows what a spiral galaxy in the Antlia Constellation looked like long ago. The Milky Way is also a spiral galaxy.

Stars in other galaxies are very far away. It can take billions of years for their light to reach Earth. By the time their light is visible to us, these stars might no longer exist. They may have collapsed or exploded in space.

Although we cannot travel back in time, scientists have found a way for us to look back in time. Using telescopes, astronomers can take pictures of stars whose light has just now reached our solar system. Some of these stars are 12 million **light-years** away. That means we are looking 12 million years into the past.

The Year

By observing the movements of the Sun and other objects in the sky, people began to mark the passing of time. The Sun is at the center of our solar system. It is how we measure time on Earth. The Sun's **gravity** pulls all of the planets around it on **elliptical**, or oval, paths called orbits.

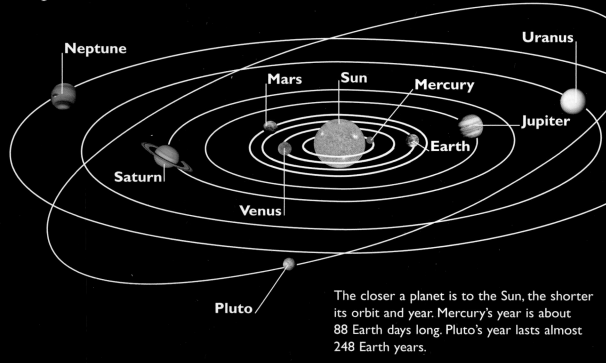

The closer a planet is to the Sun, the shorter its orbit and year. Mercury's year is about 88 Earth days long. Pluto's year lasts almost 248 Earth years.

Each planet's year is measured by how long it takes that planet to make one complete orbit of the Sun. This period of time is called the solar year. Earth takes about 365¼ days to orbit the Sun, so Earth's solar year is about 365¼ days long. Calendars today mark most years as only 365 days long. What happens to those extra quarter days? Every four years, one day, February 29, is added to the year. This year is called a leap year.

The Month

Ancient peoples watched the Moon change its shape from a full Moon to a new Moon to a full Moon again. These changes are known as the **phases of the Moon**. The 29½ days it takes for the Moon to go through all of its phases is called a lunar month. The word *lunar* means "of the Moon," and the word *month* comes from the word *moon*. A lunar year consists of twelve lunar months. This adds up to 354 days—eleven days less than a solar year. The solar calendar today uses twelve months, each having twenty-eight to thirty-one days. The longer months cover the additional eleven days that were not included in the lunar year.

Phases of the Moon

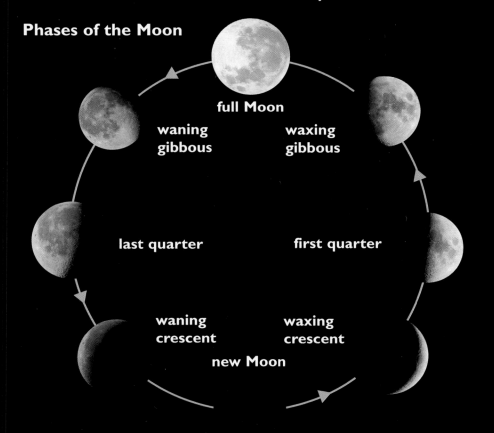

full Moon

waning gibbous

waxing gibbous

last quarter

first quarter

waning crescent

waxing crescent

new Moon

Night and Day

When it is morning in New York, it is night in Melbourne, Australia. This is because Earth spins on its **axis**. As it spins, the side of Earth facing the Sun has daytime. The opposite side has nighttime. Earth takes 24 hours to spin all the way around its axis. People use this time to determine the length of one day.

About 5,000 years ago, the Babylonians divided a day into twenty-four sections. They decided that there would be 60 minutes in an hour and 60 seconds in a minute. People are not sure why the Babylonians used sixty as a base number. Some think it is because sixty is divisible by so many numbers. Others think that it was because the Babylonians thought the number six was important.

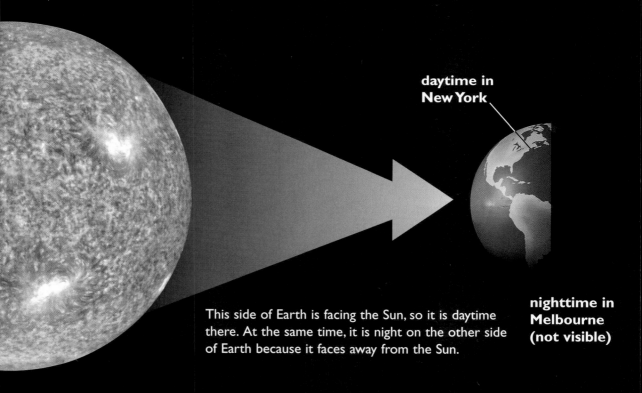

daytime in New York

nighttime in Melbourne (not visible)

This side of Earth is facing the Sun, so it is daytime there. At the same time, it is night on the other side of Earth because it faces away from the Sun.

The number of hours of daylight in a day changes over the course of a year. Some days have more hours of daylight than others. It depends on the time of year and location. Earth is tilted on its axis as it orbits the Sun. The number of daylight hours in a particular place is based on the orientation of Earth's tilt. When a hemisphere is tilted away from the Sun, it has fewer hours of daylight. When it is tilted toward the Sun, it has more hours of daylight. When one hemisphere has the most possible hours of daylight and the other has the fewest, it is called a **solstice**. Solstices happen twice a year.

In March and September, both hemispheres have an **equinox**. The equinox is when the Sun is directly over the **equator**. On these days, daylight and nighttime are of equal length throughout the world.

In the polar regions there are times when the Sun does not set at all. This phenomenon is called the Midnight Sun. During these times, children can play soccer long after it would normally be dark in other countries.

11

The Seasons

People have also used the seasons as a way to measure time during a year. Ancient peoples observed the changes in seasonal weather. In many places, a hot summer leads to a cool autumn. This is followed by a cold winter and then a warm spring. Predictable patterns, repeated year after year, helped people decide when to plant crops or store food for winter.

Not all places on Earth have the same seasons at the same time. As Earth makes its way around the Sun, it rotates around an axis, an imaginary line joining the North Pole, the center of Earth, and the South Pole. The way the axis is tilted determines how strong the Sun's rays are in a particular place at a particular time. It is what causes the seasons.

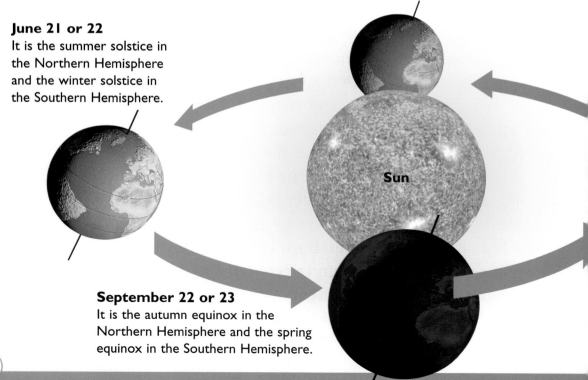

March 20 or 21
It is the spring equinox in the Northern Hemisphere and the autumn equinox in the Southern Hemisphere.

June 21 or 22
It is the summer solstice in the Northern Hemisphere and the winter solstice in the Southern Hemisphere.

Sun

September 22 or 23
It is the autumn equinox in the Northern Hemisphere and the spring equinox in the Southern Hemisphere.

Hallstatt, Austria

Sydney, Australia

February brings warm weather to Australia and snow to Austria.

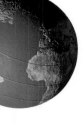
December 21 or 22
It is the winter solstice in the Northern Hemisphere and the summer solstice in the Southern Hemisphere.

It is summer in the Northern Hemisphere when the North Pole is tilted toward the Sun. At the same time, the Southern Hemisphere is tilted away from the Sun and has winter. So, while it is summer in North America and Europe, it is winter in Australia.

As Earth continues its orbit around the Sun, the seasons change. The Northern Hemisphere is tilted away from the Sun and has short winter days, while the Southern Hemisphere has long summer days. How many hours of daylight occur during each day in any place on Earth is determined by where Earth is in its orbit around the Sun.

Some places do not have four distinct seasons. Near the equator, Earth's tilt has little effect on the amount of sunlight. So the seasons there are more often marked by changes in weather patterns, such as the start of a wet season or a dry season, rather than by temperature changes.

Organizing Time

Time Zones

Different places on Earth face the Sun at different times as Earth rotates on its axis. To deal with this difference, the world has been divided into twenty-four separate time zones. Time zones were created in the United States and Canada in the 1880s. Railroad managers realized that their schedules needed a single time standard so cross-country travelers would not become confused by local times in small towns. By 1883, railroad managers in the United States had divided the country into four time zones.

When it is 7:00 A.M. (07:00) in Toronto, what time is it in Melbourne?

World Time Zone Map

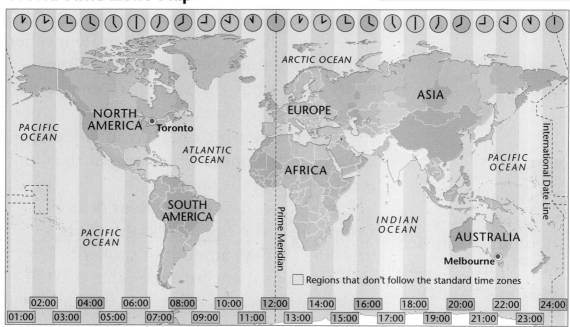

This map shows the world's twenty-four time zones. The time is measured in twenty-four hours, from one midnight to the next. Some large countries are in two time zones and have to choose which time to follow.

In 1884, at an international conference held in Washington, D.C., Earth was divided into twenty-four time zones, with Greenwich, England, serving as the first one, known as the "zero zone."

The lines of **longitude** that divide the time zones run from the North Pole to the South Pole. These imaginary lines are also called **meridians**. Usually, the time zone changes at the meridians, which occur about every 15 degrees. (Here, a degree is a measure of distance, not temperature.) However, sometimes the lines marking different time zones zigzag.

The zero meridian, also called the **Prime Meridian**, marks the center of the zero zone. All clocks are based on the time there, which is called Greenwich Mean Time, or GMT. Moving east of the Prime Meridian, each time zone is one hour later than the previous zone. If it is noon in Greenwich, it is 1:00 P.M. (13:00) in the next time zone to the east. West of the Prime Meridian, each zone is an hour earlier than the one before. If it is noon in Greenwich, it is 11:00 A.M. (11:00) in the first time zone west of Greenwich.

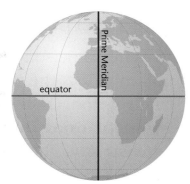

This globe shows the Prime Meridian and the equator. The vertical blue lines are lines of longitude, and the horizontal blue lines are lines of latitude.

The Prime Meridian in Greenwich, England, is marked by an illuminated green line at night.

The International Date Line

When a person travels from one time zone to the next, not only does the time change but sometimes the date changes, too. Once someone travels across the **International Date Line**, the traveler will be in a different day. The International Date Line is located for the most part along the 180 degrees meridian, halfway around the world from the Greenwich meridian. In some places the International Date Line zigzags or bulges. It does this so that small countries can have only one time zone, when a meridian would split the land into two zones.

The last change to the date line was made in 1995 so that all of the Kiribati island group could be in the same day at the same time. Kiribati's Caroline Island is located just west of the date line boundary and so became the first place on Earth to see in the year 2000. It was renamed Millennium Island in 1999 to mark the event.

The International Date Line

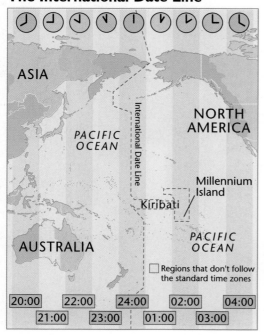

The International Date Line does not run in a straight line. If it did, some countries would experience two days at the same time. You can see more clearly how the date line relates to the world's time zones by looking back at the map on page 14.

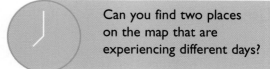

Can you find two places on the map that are experiencing different days?

Fred's Journey

Let's follow a traveler named Fred, who is about to leave Hawaii to visit the Philippines. To get to the Philippines, Fred must travel west and cross the International Date Line.

If Fred leaves Hawaii on Tuesday morning, it is already Wednesday in the Philippines. Traveling west across the International Date Line means that he will lose a day.

However, when Fred leaves the Philippines to return to Hawaii, he will have to travel across the International Date Line again. This means that he gains a day. Depending on the time his plane takes off, if he leaves the Philippines on Thursday, he may arrive in Hawaii on Wednesday—the day before he set out!

When Fred crosses the International Date Line, he moves into a new time zone and a new day.

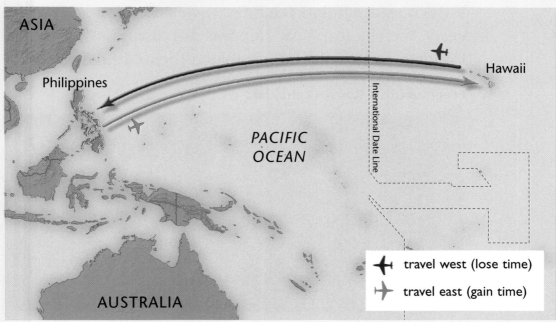

ASIA

Philippines

PACIFIC OCEAN

International Date Line

Hawaii

AUSTRALIA

✈ travel west (lose time)

✈ travel east (gain time)

Measuring Time

Measuring the Year

The first calendars were made to help people remember the dates of events that were important to them. Usually these calendars were based on either lunar year or solar year cycles. After a few years passed, however, these calendars would not match up with the seasons. So, people dropped or added days or months to fit with the cycle of the seasons.

The Romans used a ten-month calendar, which didn't add up to the 365¼ days of the solar year. So they added two months to follow the lunar calendar and also inserted an extra month every other year.

In 46 B.C., the Roman emperor, Julius Caesar, established a solar calendar with twelve months. Known as the Julian calendar, it was used for 1,500 years, but the leap-year rule was not always followed. Holidays eventually did not match their original seasons.

Fragment of a Roman calendar

The Romans called the first day of each month *calends*, which means "to call out." This is where our word *calendar* comes from.

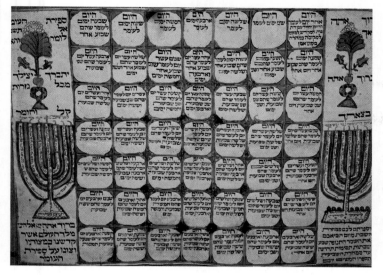

The Hebrew calendar is based on both the Sun and the Moon. It is used by Jews worldwide to determine, among other things, the start of the new Hebrew month and when the Jewish holidays are. Every month starts (approximately) on the day of a new Moon.

In 1582, Pope Gregory XIII created a new calendar. First, to balance the calendar with the seasons, he removed ten days. For the first year only, the calendar skipped from October 4 to October 15. This new Gregorian calendar, which added a leap year once every four years, is still in use today.

Another calendar is the Hebrew calendar. It is like the Gregorian calendar, but instead of having a leap year, it has a thirteenth month every few years. This calendar was developed and first used more than 3,000 years ago. That means that the year 2010 would be 5770–5771 on the Hebrew calendar. Other calendars were also developed within the Chinese, Indian, Islamic, Aztec, and Mayan cultures.

The Aztec calendar was based on the Sun. This Aztec calendar stone has the Sun God at its center.

Measuring the Day

Clocks help measure time in much smaller units than calendars. The first timepieces were made about 4,000 years ago. They were not very accurate. The Babylonians were the first to divide daylight time into twelve units of time. No one is exactly sure why the Babylonians chose twelve.

Objects in sunlight cast shadows of different lengths and at different angles throughout the day. Early clocks that used the Sun used large objects, such as pyramids, or smaller sticks or poles, to cast a shadow that could be tracked. People could tell the time by looking at the shadow's length and angle. This method of telling time led to the invention of sundials by the Babylonians. The shadow cast by a pointer would move across the sundial surface, which was marked with lines to show the hours of the day.

The markings on a sundial show us what time it is.

This large structure is the sundial's pointer.

The largest sundial in the world is in Jaipur, India. It is part of an outdoor observatory, which has many giant instruments for watching the sky.

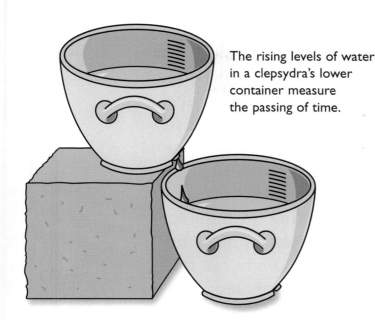

The rising levels of water in a clepsydra's lower container measure the passing of time.

Another type of clepsydra is a single container with a hole from which water escapes. The decreasing levels of water inside measure the passing of time. The one above is from ancient Egypt.

Water clocks were used in ancient Greece and Egypt thousands of years ago. A water clock is also called a **clepsydra** (KLEHP-sih-druh). Unlike sundials, a clepsydra could show the time indoors or at night. Water dripped at a constant rate from one container to another. The markings on the bottom container were used to measure the hours that passed as it filled. One use for clepsydras was to time speeches in law courts.

The hourglass is another timepiece used thousands of years ago. It was similar to the clepsydra, but it used sand. The sand flowed from one section of a glass container to another. The special shape of the glass allowed sand to pass through at a steady rate. The amount of sand in the bottom of the glass showed how much time had passed.

An hourglass uses sand to measure passing time. It takes one hour for the sand to completely run from the top to the bottom of this hourglass.

21

Mechanical Clocks

The tick-tock sound of a clock was first heard when people started making mechanical clocks. We do not know exactly who invented the first mechanical clocks. Some people believe they were invented in Europe in the late 1200s or early 1300s. Mechanical clocks used weights or springs, which could be easily damaged, so they were not always very accurate.

By the 1500s, people were making small, portable clocks, called pocket watches. These signified a big change in time telling—people could now tell time wherever they were. People were also making other kinds of clocks, and these clocks were often very large. Some were made of iron and weighed several tons.

History of Mechanical Clocks

Salisbury Cathedral clock

seventeenth-century portable clock

pendulum clock

1386	**1510**	**1657**
The world's oldest surviving mechanical clock is built at Salisbury Cathedral in southern England. It is still working today.	The first spring-powered clocks are made by Peter Henlein, a German locksmith. They are very light and can be carried easily.	The first pendulum clock is made by Christiaan Huygens, a Dutch astronomer.

About a hundred years later, pendulum clocks were invented. The pendulum swings from left to right in a constant motion. This feature made pendulum clocks more reliable than previous clocks. They were inaccurate by only a few seconds each day.

In 1735, clocks became even more accurate. Until then, it had been especially hard to tell time aboard a ship. The rocking of the ship on the waves interfered with the swings of a clock's pendulum, causing the clock to be inaccurate. This led one man, John Harrison, to invent the **marine chronometer**. The chronometer worked using a balance spring with two weights. The weights enabled the chronometer to keep accurate time regardless of the rocking of the ship.

traditional cuckoo clock

Harrison 4 marine chronometer

Big Ben

1730	1759	1859
Cuckoo clocks are first used in Germany. Cuckoo clocks use a pendulum and weights to keep time.	John Harrison makes an accurate timekeeper for people at sea. It is his fourth attempt at making one and is called the Harrison 4.	Big Ben is built. It sits atop the Houses of Parliament in London, England. The name at first only referred to the bell that strikes the hour.

Digital Time

Today, many clocks do not have springs or pendulums. They run on electricity or batteries.

Digital clocks have an electronic counter instead of gears, like traditional clocks have. Many also have a very small quartz crystal inside. When powered by a battery, the crystal vibrates. If the clock has hands, the crystal's pulse causes these hands to move. Most of today's watches also use a quartz crystal.

Many electric clocks and watches don't have hands. They have what is called an LCD, a liquid crystal display, or an LED, a light emitting diode. The time is shown in numerals.

quartz crystal

LCD

battery

LED

Digital timepieces were revolutionary when they first appeared in the 1970s, but they are now an everyday sight.

Mechanical clocks are still in use, but most clocks and watches today are electric and don't need to be wound.

The clocks that are most accurate at keeping time are atomic clocks. They don't use a spring, a pendulum, or a quartz crystal. Atomic clocks count the steady vibrations of an **atom**, which is the smallest part of an element. These beats are very dependable. Atoms can vibrate more than 9 billion times a second. Since 1967, atomic clocks have been used to keep the official time throughout the world. It can take millions of years before an atomic clock is inaccurate by even one second.

The future might bring many new ways to measure time. New technology will probably introduce even more accurate clocks and calendars. People will always be running to meet trains, checking to see when a soccer game starts, and listening for the bell to signal the end of a test or some other event. No matter what new timepieces we have, people will still be asking, "What time is it?"

The first atomic clock was made in the United States. It used an ammonia molecule as the source of vibrations.

These two pages show the history of life on Earth as if it had all happened in one 24-hour day, starting at midnight and continuing until it is midnight again. Instead of years, here the world's history is measured in hours.

Looking at these clocks, you can see when Earth was formed. They show when various life forms first appeared on Earth and how long dinosaurs were on Earth before human beings appeared.

6:30 A.M.

In this model, Earth was created at 12:00 A.M. However, the first living organisms did not appear until about 6:30 A.M.

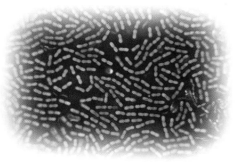

Bacteria are among the earliest life forms.

9:15 P.M.

Fishes appeared at 9:15 P.M.

The coelacanth is a direct descendant of prehistoric fish.

10:50 P.M.

Dinosaurs appeared on Earth at 10:50 P.M. but were extinct by 11:40 P.M.

This is a fossil of a Tyrannosaurus rex.

11:00 P.M.

This clock shows 11:00 P.M., the time when mammals first appeared.

Early mammals looked similar to this modern shrew.

11:59 P.M.

Humans first walked on Earth in the last 40 seconds before midnight. All of the rest of human civilization from ancient days until today is squeezed into the very last 0.1 second on the clock.

Questions About Time

Is time travel possible?

There are theories that if we were able to move faster than the speed of light, or could travel through wormholes in space, we might be able to travel back in time. These ideas have been used in many exciting television shows and movies, but many scientists believe that they would be impossible to do. However, it may be that we will understand these things better in the future—only time will tell...

How can you tell which years will be leap years?

Leap years occur in every year that can be divided evenly by four. However, to keep the calendar in line with the time it takes for Earth to orbit the Sun, the only century years that are leap years are those that can be divided by 400.

Why do we need to measure time so precisely?

Many people have jobs that depend on knowing the precise time. For example, a ship's navigator finds longitude by comparing the time on a chronometer with local time.

Timeline of Timekeeping

1500 B.C.	early 1300s (A.D.)	1657	1730–1735
sundial used by ancient Egyptians and Greeks	first mechanical clocks	first pendulum clocks	first marine chronometers

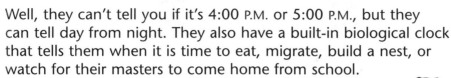

 How do animals know what time it is?

Well, they can't tell you if it's 4:00 P.M. or 5:00 P.M., but they can tell day from night. They also have a built-in biological clock that tells them when it is time to eat, migrate, build a nest, or watch for their masters to come home from school.

migrating geese

 What's a body clock?

A body, or biological, clock is the automatic system in humans and other animals that controls the cycles of sleeping and waking. Your body clock is what wakes you up in the morning and what makes you feel sleepy at night.

 How can you tell the time if you don't have a clock?

Some people, such as farmers, spend much of their time outdoors. These people can often tell the time quite accurately without a clock. From long experience, they learn to judge the time from the position of the Sun in the sky. Noon occurs when the Sun reaches its highest point in the sky. Times in the morning and afternoon can be estimated by the angle of the Sun above the horizon.

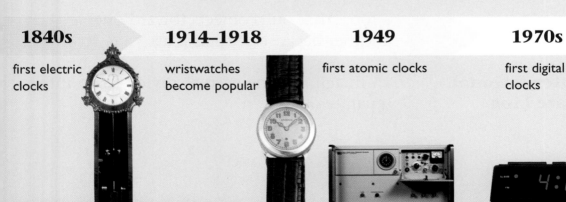

1840s
first electric clocks

1914–1918
wristwatches become popular

1949
first atomic clocks

1970s
first digital clocks

29

Glossary

atom   the smallest particle of an element

atomic clocks   extremely accurate clocks that use the vibrations of atoms to keep time

axis   an imaginary line running through the center of Earth from the North Pole to the South Pole

Big Bang   the term used to describe the theory on the explosive birth of the universe between 10 and 15 billion years ago

clepsydra   an ancient water clock

elliptical   oval shaped

equator   an imaginary line around Earth that is the same distance from the North and South poles and divides Earth into the Northern and Southern hemispheres

equinox   when the Sun is directly over the equator

gravity   a force that pulls objects toward one another because of their mass

International Date Line   an imaginary line used to divide Earth into separate days

light-year	the distance light travels in one year
longitude	imaginary lines around Earth that run from the North Pole to the South Pole measuring how far east or west a place is on Earth, compared to the Prime Meridian
marine chronometer	a type of clock powered by springs that uses a balance spring and two weights to keep accurate time on a ship at sea
meridians	lines of longitude
phases of the Moon	the different shapes of the sunlit parts of the Moon as seen from Earth during the Moon's 29½ day orbit
Prime Meridian	the imaginary line that runs around Earth from the North Pole to the South Pole, through Greenwich, England, and marks 0 degrees longitude
solstice	when the Sun is overhead at its northernmost and southernmost points in the sky

Index